D0099604

from SEA TO SHINING SEA

DELAWARE

By Dennis Brindell Fradin and Judith Bloom Fradin

CONSULTANTS

Constance J. Cooper, Ph.D., Manuscript Librarian, Historical Society of Delaware

Robert L. Hillerich, Ph.D., Professor Emeritus, Bowling Green State University;
Consultant, Pinellas County Schools, Florida

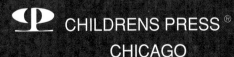

CP CHILDRENS PRESS ®
CHICAGO

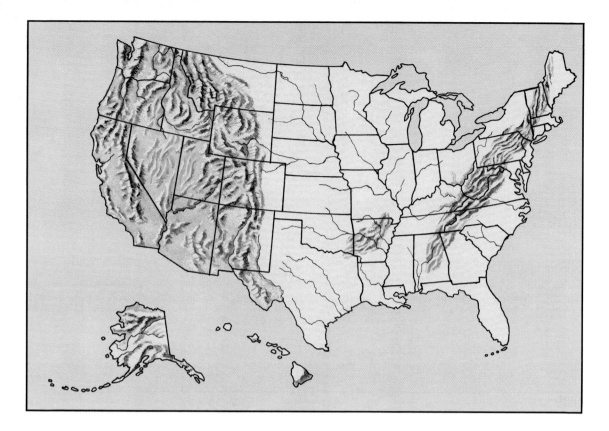

Delaware is one of the fourteen states in the region called the South. The other southern states are Alabama, Arkansas, Florida, Georgia, Kentucky, Louisiana, Maryland, Mississippi, North Carolina, South Carolina, Tennessee, Virginia, and West Virginia.

For our aunt and uncle, Anne and Milton Colman

Front cover picture: Wilmington; page 1: A New Castle County farm; back cover: Winterthur Gardens in the spring

Project Editor: Joan Downing
Design Director: Karen Kohn
Typesetting: Graphic Connections, Inc.
Engraving: Liberty Photoengraving

Library of Congress Cataloging-in-Publication Data

Fradin, Dennis B.
  Delaware / by Dennis Brindell Fradin & Judith Bloom
Fradin.
    p.   cm. — (From sea to shining sea)
  Includes index.
  ISBN 0-516-03808-7
  1. Delaware—Juvenile literature. [1. Delaware.]
I. Fradin, Judith Bloom. II. Title. III. Series: Fradin,
Dennis B. From sea to shining sea.
F164.3.F69   1995   94-35022
975.1—dc20   CIP
                                              AC

Table of Contents

Children enjoying a Fourth of July celebration

Introducing the First State

Only Rhode Island is smaller than Delaware. Alaska, the largest state, is almost 290 times Delaware's size.

Delaware lies along the East Coast of the United States. It is one of the southern states. Delaware is also the second smallest of the fifty states. Although small, Delaware has a grand history. Swedish and Dutch people were its first European settlers. Later, Delaware became one of England's thirteen colonies. As a state, it was the first to accept the United States Constitution. That is why Delaware is nicknamed the "First State."

Today, Delaware is sometimes called the "Company State." Thousands of America's biggest companies were formed there. Many large chemical companies are located in Wilmington. That is Delaware's biggest city.

Delaware is also a rich farming state. The raising of broiler chickens started there. Peas, soybeans, and milk are other leading farm goods.

Delaware is special in many other ways. Where were the country's first log cabins built? Where was astronomer Annie Jump Cannon born? Where was nylon invented? The answer to these questions is the First State: Delaware!

A picture map
of Delaware

Overleaf: Reflections
on the pond, Lums
Pond State Park

5

Coastal Plain, Woods, and Waterways

Coastal Plain, Woods, and Waterways

Delaware covers 2,044 square miles. It is the smallest of the southern states. Delaware shares the Delmarva Peninsula with parts of two other southern states. The peninsula's name came from the names of the states on it: *Delaware, Maryland,* and *Virginia.*

Cypress trees in Trussum Pond, near Pepper

On a map, Delaware looks like an elf's shoe. The toe curves north against Pennsylvania. Its sole pushes west against Maryland. To the south, the heel rests against Maryland, also. To the east, three bodies of water form the shoe's top: the Delaware River, Delaware Bay, and the Atlantic Ocean. New Jersey lies farther east across the river and bay.

Most of Delaware is low, flat coastal plain. One-sixth of the state is made up of wetlands. On the southern border lies Cypress Swamp, also known as the Great Pocomoke Swamp. Along the bay and ocean are sand dunes and beaches. Many islands dot Delaware's shoreline. The largest are Pea Patch, Reedy, and Fenwick islands. A slice of far northern Delaware is part of the Piedmont. This is hilly land with rich river valleys. Delaware's tallest point is in the Piedmont. It stands only 442 feet high.

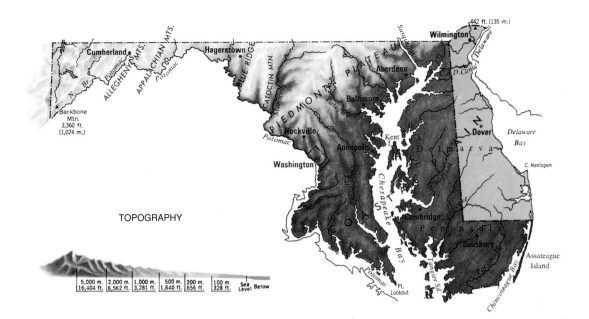

TOPOGRAPHY

5,000 m. | 2,000 m. | 1,000 m. | 500 m. | 200 m. | 100 m. | Sea | Below
16,404 ft. | 6,562 ft. | 3,281 ft. | 1,640 ft. | 656 ft. | 328 ft. | Level |

WOODS, WILDLIFE, AND WATERWAYS

One-third of Delaware is woodland. The American holly is the state tree. It has bright red berries. Pine, hickory, oak, willow, wild cherry, and cedar trees also grow there. Many wild plants grow in Delaware's woods and swamps. Mistletoe grows on sweet gum trees. Swamp magnolias, blueberries, and water lilies are other wild plants in Delaware.

Deer are Delaware's largest wild animals. Foxes, beavers, rabbits, muskrats, and otters also live there. Snapping turtles are found in some wetlands. Horseshoe crabs lay their eggs in Delaware Bay. These animals are not really crabs. They are more

Horseshoe crabs and laughing gulls share a Delaware Bay beach. The gulls are looking for the eggs just laid by the crabs.

9

like spiders. Delaware's state fish is the weakfish. It grows to be about 2 feet long. The weakfish lives in shallow ocean waters. Clams, crabs, sturgeon, and bass also live in Delaware waters. Woodpeckers, orioles, and blue jays fly about the state. Snowy egrets and blue herons can be spotted near water.

Delaware has about fifty small lakes. Lums Pond is the largest. It covers just one-third of a square mile. The Delaware is the state's main river. This 300-mile river begins in New York. The Christina, Smyrna, St. Jones, Broadkill, and Nanticoke are other important rivers. Brandywine Creek flows through northern Delaware.

A great blue heron

CLIMATE

A winter scene at Wooddale Bridge in Hockessin

The First State has a warm, wet climate. Summer temperatures of 80 degrees Fahrenheit are common. Summer ocean breezes keep the seacoast cooler than inland areas. This helps make the beaches popular.

On most winter days, Delaware temperatures top 40 degrees Fahrenheit. Mountains to the west shield Delaware from cold winds. The ocean to the east helps warm the state in winter. Snowfall is usually light. About 18 inches fall in the north each year. Southern Delaware receives about 14 inches of snow.

From Ancient Times Until Today

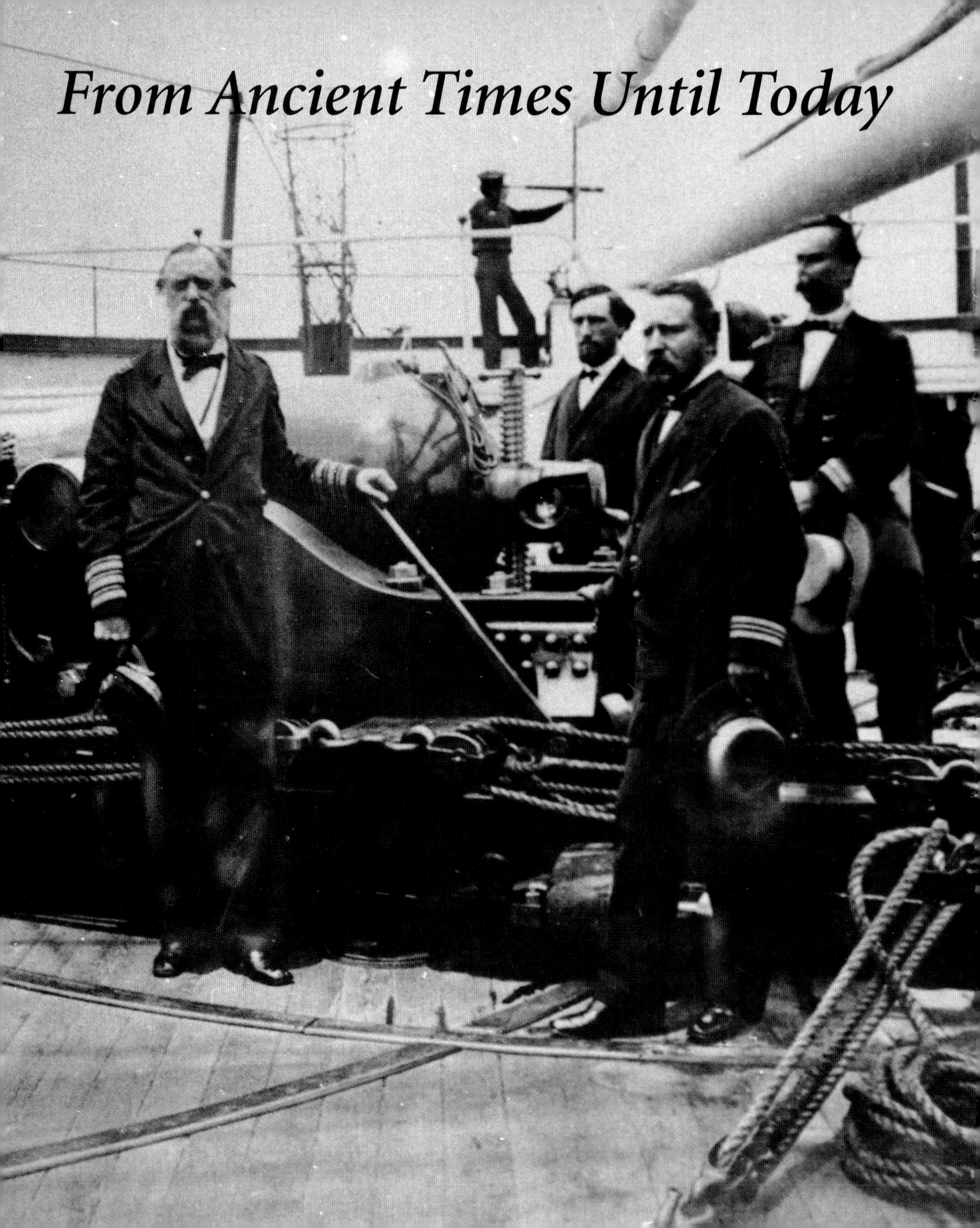

FROM ANCIENT TIMES UNTIL TODAY

Millions of years ago, the ocean covered most of Delaware. Octopuses and giant snails once lived there. Their fossils have been found in the state.

Opposite: Admiral Samuel Francis du Pont (on the left) helped the North control the seacoast during the Civil War.

AMERICAN INDIANS

Indians lived in places near Delaware more than 10,000 years ago. So it is likely that they were in Delaware at that time, too. The oldest Indian remains found in Delaware are 1,500 years old. They include bones, tools, and bowls.

Several groups of Indians came to Delaware. The Nanticokes, Choptanks, and Assateagues lived in the south and west. The main Indian group called themselves the Lenape. This meant "First People" or "Our People." They lived along the Delaware River.

Lenape villages had about 100 people. Their homes were wigwams. They were built of wood and bark. Near these homes, Lenape women and children grew corn, beans, and squash. The men and their older sons hunted and fished. Succotash was a

Tish-Co-Han, a Delaware chief

13

Swedish settlers arrived in Delaware in 1638.

popular dish. The Lenape made it by mixing corn and beans. Their children enjoyed a candy made of maple sugar and cornmeal.

The Lenape held ceremonies during the year. These included the Corn Dance and Harvest Festival. They honored the Lenape's gods. The Lenape were a peaceful people. Other Indian groups asked them to settle disputes. Some Indians called the Lenape "Our Grandfathers" out of respect. Later, English settlers called them the "Delaware."

European Explorers and Settlers

In 1610, an English ship sailed into Delaware Bay. England had already settled the colony of Virginia

14

to the south. The ship's captain named the bay after Virginia's governor. He was Lord De La Warr. Soon after that, the bay, river, and land were called Delaware.

A year earlier, Henry Hudson had explored Delaware Bay for The Netherlands. Hudson was from England. Delaware's beauty impressed him. He reported seeing "a white sandy shore and within it green trees."

In 1631, the Dutch built a settlement along Delaware's southeast coast. It was called Zwaanendael. That means "Valley of the Swans" in Dutch. But the newcomers did not get along with the Indians. By mid-1632, the Indians had destroyed the settlement.

Sweden, too, claimed Delaware. In 1638, two Swedish ships brought colonists to northeast Delaware. They anchored on a river that they named the Christina. It was named for Sweden's twelve-year-old queen. Along the river, they built Fort Christina. This outpost was Delaware's first lasting European settlement. It was built at the site of what is now the city of Wilmington.

The Swedes also claimed land in New Jersey and Pennsylvania. They called their American land New Sweden. People from Sweden and neighboring

The Zwaanendael Museum in Lewes was built to mark the 300th anniversary of Delaware's first Dutch settlement in 1631. Dutch refers to the people and language of The Netherlands.

A replica of a Swedish log cabin at Fort Christina

Finland settled in New Sweden. In Delaware, they built America's first log cabins.

In 1643, Johan Printz arrived at Fort Christina. He came to govern New Sweden. Printz weighed over 400 pounds. The Indians nicknamed him "Big Belly." Under his leadership, forts and trading posts were built in New Sweden. The settlers traded with the Indians for furs. The furs were shipped to Sweden. Cloth makers, bakers, and millers set up businesses in Delaware. However, New Sweden's population never topped 1,000.

During this same time, the Dutch claimed land called New Netherland. It included New York and New Jersey. The Dutch wanted to add Delaware to New Netherland. In 1651, they built Fort Casimir. It was the beginning of New Castle. In 1655, the Dutch captured New Sweden without a fight. Delaware then became part of New Netherland.

But the Dutch had the same problem as the Swedes. Few Dutch settlers went to Delaware. By 1660, Delaware still had fewer than 1,000 settlers.

AN ENGLISH COLONY

England, meanwhile, had settled many colonies north and south of New Netherland. In 1664,

England seized New Netherland. England then ruled most of the East Coast. From 1682 to 1704, Delaware was part of England's Pennsylvania colony. Delaware was known as Pennsylvania's "Three Lower Counties." In 1704, the Three Lower Counties were granted their own legislature.

Delaware grew under English rule. Newark was settled in the early 1700s. Dover was founded in 1717. Many English Quakers moved to Delaware. The members of this faith opposed war and slavery. They also believed that all people were equal. Quakers helped settle Wilmington, near the site of Fort Christina, in the 1730s. Wilmington became a

The king of England gave Pennsylvania, including the Three Lower Counties, to Quaker William Penn. Penn arrived in Pennsylvania in 1682.

In 1664, England took New Netherland from the Dutch. Peter Stuyvesant (with cane) surrendered New Amsterdam.

flour-milling center. Sawmills went up along Delaware's rivers. They turned logs into lumber. The lumber was used to build new towns and homes. By 1760, Delaware had about 35,000 people.

THE REVOLUTIONARY WAR

In the 1760s and 1770s, England placed taxes on the American colonies. Many colonists refused to pay the taxes. Delawareans participated in the protests. In 1775, the Americans went to war against England. This was called the Revolutionary War (1775-1783).

A statue of Caesar Rodney

During the war, delegates from the thirteen colonies met in Philadelphia, Pennsylvania. Delaware had three delegates: George Read, Thomas McKean, and Caesar Rodney. McKean and Rodney favored independence from England. Read did not. For Delaware to choose independence, two of the three delegates had to vote for it. The vote on that matter was set for July 2, 1776. On July 1, Rodney was still in Dover. He had stopped an uprising of Delawareans who sided with England. Riding 80 miles through a stormy night, Rodney reached Philadelphia on July 2. He swung Delaware's vote for independence.

On July 4, 1776, the delegates issued the Declaration of Independence. Thomas Jefferson wrote the declaration. Through it, the thirteen colonies became the United States of America. Delaware's delegates, including Read, signed it. Jefferson called Delaware the "Diamond State." Although it was small, Delaware was of great value.

In June 1776, Delaware had broken from Pennsylvania. In August, it became the Delaware State. Delaware was the first of the old colonies to call itself a state. Delawareans called their first governors "presidents."

Only one Revolutionary War battle took place in Delaware. The Battle of Cooch's Bridge was fought near Newark on September 3, 1777. The British won that battle. But Delawareans helped win battles elsewhere. One Delaware officer is said to have carried fighting roosters into battle. These birds were called the "Blue Hen's Chickens." Their mother was a bluish hen. Delaware men fought bravely. They, too, became known as the "Blue Hen's Chickens." Some reportedly went into battle yelling, "We're sons of the Blue Hen, and we're game to the end!"

The war ended in 1783. The United States had become a free and independent country.

More than 3,500 Delawareans fought for independence.

Some people still raise Blue hen chickens. Their feathers give them the bluish look. The Blue hen chicken became the state bird long after statehood.

The First State

In 1787, America's leaders again met in Philadelphia. That time they wrote the United States Constitution. The Constitution became the framework for the new country's government. By accepting the Constitution, each state became part of the United States. Delaware was the first state to do so. On December 7, 1787, Delaware became the first state in the Union. Delawareans were nicknamed the Blue Hen's Chickens.

Many people in the young state farmed. Industry also gained importance. In 1795, Jacob Broom built a cotton mill on Brandywine Creek. Broom helped cloth making become important in Delaware.

Du Pont workers at the plant near Wilmington about 1900

In 1801, Éleuthère Irénée du Pont moved from France to Delaware. He began a gunpowder mill on Brandywine Creek near Wilmington in 1802. The Eleutherian Mills were the start of the Du Pont Company. Du Pont became the world's biggest chemical-making company. Wilmington became known as the "Chemical Capital of the World."

In 1817, Thomas Gilpin made the country's first modern papermaking machine. Papermaking became a big Delaware business. So did shipbuilding and shipping. New people came to work in Delaware's factories. By 1850, the First State's population was 91,532.

THE FIGHT OVER SLAVERY

Rich Delaware landowners bought African slaves. The slaves did the work on the landowners' big farms. Slavery had been allowed in Delaware since the 1640s. The other southern states also had slavery. By 1850, Delawareans had only about 2,300 slaves. Another 18,000 black Delawareans were free.

Delaware's Quakers hated slavery. Some of them helped slaves escape along the Underground Railroad. This was a series of hiding places. Slaves used them on their way north to freedom. The

Shipbuilding became a big Delaware business in the 1800s. This 1892 picture shows the hull of the SS J.G. Christopher, a ship that was built by the Jackson & Sharp Company.

21

Quaker iron merchant Thomas Garrett (above) helped thousands of slaves escape to the North.

A Civil War re-enactment on Pea Patch Island

Quaker Meeting House in Odessa was an Underground Railroad "station." So was Thomas Garrett's house in Wilmington. Garrett helped more than 2,000 runaway slaves.

Slavery was one of the reasons for the Civil War (1861-1865). In that war, eleven southern states left the Union. They formed the Confederate States of America (the South). Although a southern state, Delaware remained in the Union (the North). More than 12,000 Delawareans fought for the North. Rear Admiral Samuel du Pont helped the North control the seacoast. Several hundred Delawareans fought for the South. Most of them were from Kent and Sussex counties. The North won the war in 1865. Every state had to end slavery. Delaware's few remaining slaves were then freed.

GROWTH, WORLD WARS, AND THE GREAT DEPRESSION

Delaware's legislature passed the Delaware Corporation Law in 1899. This law made it easy for people to form companies in Delaware. Other states had tighter rules and higher taxes for companies. Most of the companies did their business in other states. But they paid taxes in Delaware. This made

"AT DINNER."
Co. K 59 PIONEER INF.

Delaware very rich. Over the years, this law has brought many companies to the state.

In the early 1900s, the First State continued to grow. People from many European lands came to work there. By 1910, Delaware's population was 202,322. The next year, the Du Pont Highway was begun. This was the country's first divided highway. It now runs the complete length of Delaware.

In 1917, the United States entered World War I (1914-1918). Nearly 10,000 Delawareans helped win the war. Delaware's chemical companies supplied gunpowder. Its shipyards built many vessels.

During those years, American women were fighting for their voting rights. Delawareans Mabel

These Delaware troops of the 59th Pioneer Infantry fought on the front lines in France during World War I.

Vernon and Florence Bayard Hilles were among them. Hilles and Vernon marched on the White House in 1917. Both were arrested and jailed. But their work helped American women win the vote in 1920.

In 1923, Cecile Steele started a new business for Delaware. On her farm, she raised 500 chickens to be sold for meat. That began Delaware's broiler chicken industry. Delaware soon became a leader at raising these chickens for food.

The Great Depression (1929-1939) hurt many Delawareans. Thousands lost their jobs as factories closed. To help them, the United States government started many building projects. People in Delaware worked to make parks and to build roads.

Left: Florence B. Hilles (left) worked hard to get voting rights for women.
Right: During World War II, women not only voted, but worked at many jobs that once were held by men. These women worked at the Dravo Shipyard in Wilmington.

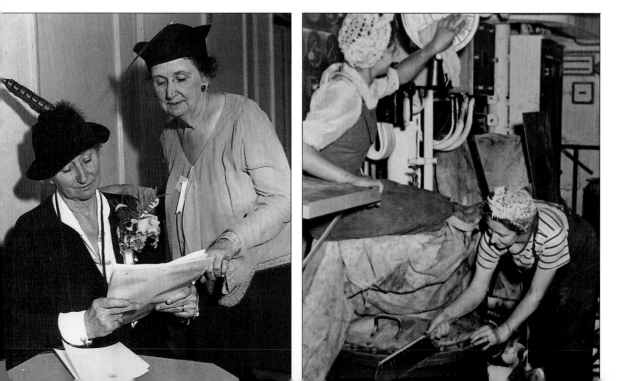

World War II (1939-1945) helped end the Great Depression. The United States entered that war in 1941. About 30,000 Delaware men and women helped win the war. Delaware's workers made ships and gunpowder. Cloth from its cotton mills became uniforms. Du Pont nylon went into parachutes. Du Pont chemist Wallace Carothers had accidentally discovered nylon in 1938.

Du Pont chemist Wallace Carothers

RECENT CHANGES

Thousands of people moved to Delaware after World War II. The state's population rose from 318,085 in 1950 to 446,292 in 1960. This was Delaware's largest ten-year population gain ever.

In 1951, travel to and from Delaware became easier. In that year, the Delaware Memorial Bridge opened. It links Delaware to New Jersey across the Delaware River.

As a southern state, Delaware had long practiced segregation. This meant that black children and white children went to separate schools. Black people and white people were not allowed to eat in the same restaurants, either. In the 1950s, Delaware started to change its laws. Black students were allowed at the University of Delaware in 1950. In

Construction of the Delaware Memorial Bridge

1952, black students and white students started attending the same high schools. Delaware ended segregation in restaurants in 1963.

During those years, many black people moved to Delaware. They came from states farther south. Most of them settled in Wilmington. At the same time, thousands of white Wilmington families moved to the suburbs.

By 1973, about 1,500 old houses stood empty in Wilmington. In that year, Wilmington began a special housing plan. For just one dollar, a person could buy an abandoned house. The new owner had to fix up the building. The plan brought many homeowners back to the city.

Wilmington's public schools had become heavily black. In 1978, Delaware made history. New Castle County became one big school district. That is where Wilmington is. Students from the city and suburbs were bused to one anothers' schools. Delaware was the first state to desegregate its schools in this way.

Growth was hurting Delaware's wetlands. The Delaware Coastal Zone Act was passed in 1971. Factories could no longer be built along the coast. Other laws protecting Delaware's beaches followed. These laws made the state more pleasing to visitors.

The 1970s also found many Delawareans out of work. Pierre S. du Pont IV was elected governor in 1976. His Financial Center Development Act passed in 1981. This law allowed out-of-state banks to have headquarters in Delaware. Soon a dozen new banks opened in the state. More than 20,000 new jobs were created. A housing boom followed. Tourism was growing by then, too. By 1993, more Delawareans had jobs than ever before. They are now among the richest Americans.

In 1787, Delawareans led the country in accepting the Constitution. Now, they see other challenges ahead. Delawareans plan to lead the country to good times in the year 2000.

Pink blossoms cover the walk in front of these historic Wilmington homes.

Overleaf: A young girl at the annual Wilmington flower market

Delawareans and Their Work

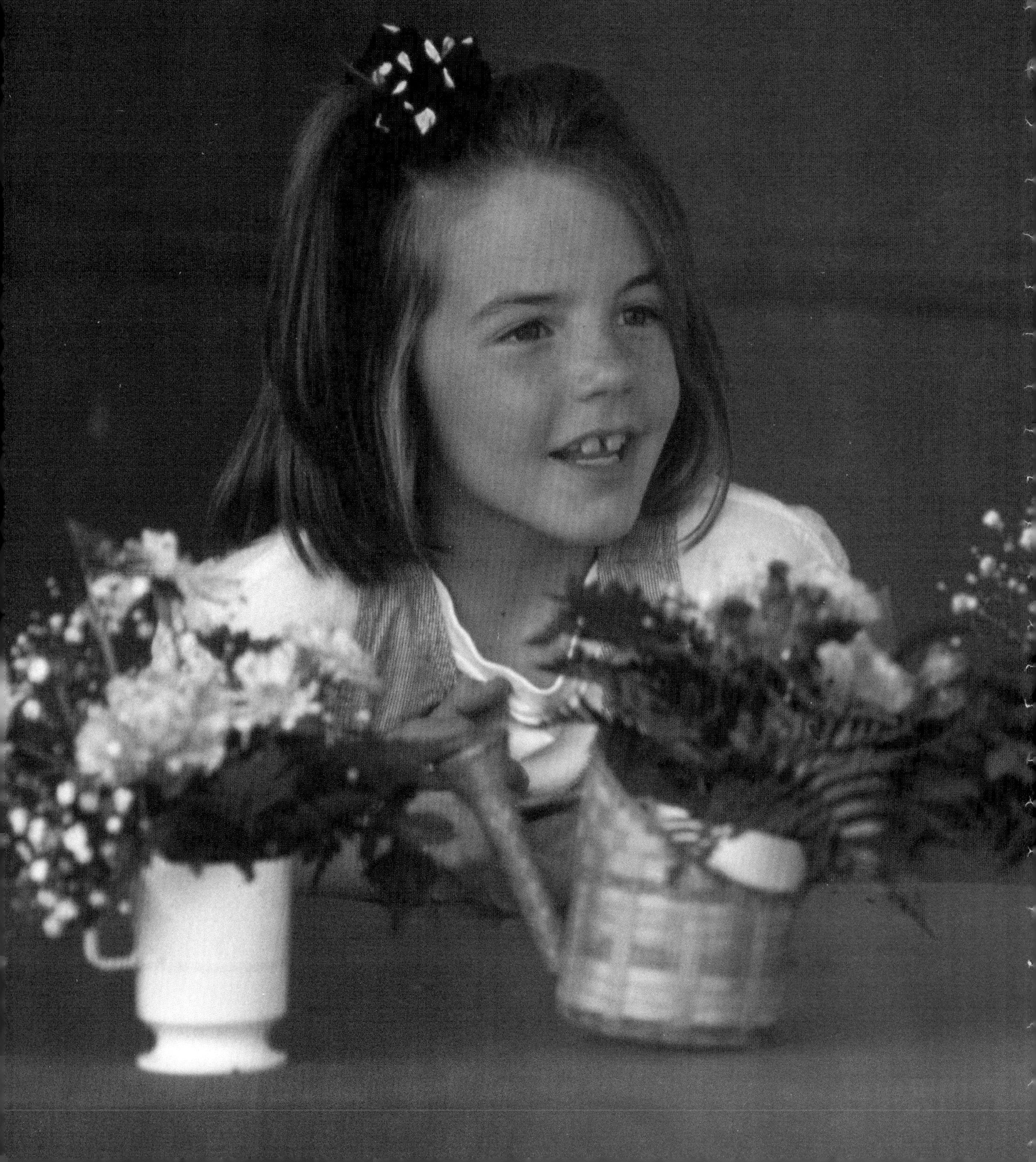

DELAWAREANS AND THEIR WORK

Delaware has 666,168 people. Only four states have fewer. About 533,000 Delawareans are white. Most of their families came from Ireland, Germany, and England. Almost 115,000 Delawareans are black. Nearly 20,000 Delawareans are Hispanic. Many of these Spanish-speaking people came from Puerto Rico. About 10,000 Asian people live in Delaware. Most of them came from India and China. About 2,000 American Indians live in the First State. The Nanticokes make up Delaware's largest Indian group.

About 2,000 Delawareans are American Indians and nearly 115,000 are black.

THEIR WORK

About 360,000 Delawareans have jobs. Service work is the state's leading kind of job. About 90,000 people are service workers. They include workers in hospitals and law offices. People who work in motels, hotels, and restaurants serve Delaware's tourists.

Selling goods employs 75,000 Delawareans. The goods range from shirts sold in tourists shops

This proud owner shows off his prize-winning Holstein at the Delaware State Fair.

Broiler chickens on their way to market

to automobiles. Nearly 70,000 Delawareans make products. Chemicals are the state's top product. The Du Pont Company makes chemicals. It is one of the top ten manufacturing companies in the United States. Nylon, plastic, and medicines are a few Delaware-made chemicals. Foods are another big Delaware product. They include packaged chicken, canned goods, and puddings. Delaware is also a large maker of cars.

Delaware has about 50,000 government workers. They include 6,000 public-school teachers. A few thousand people also work for the military. Dover Air Force Base is near the state capital.

More than 6,000 Delawareans are farmers. Broiler chickens are Delaware's top farm product.

A corn harvest near Smyrna

The state produces 225 million of these chickens a year. This nearly equals the population of the United States. Hogs and milk are other Delaware livestock products. Delaware is a leader at growing green peas. Soybeans, corn, and apples are other important crops.

Only about 200 Delawareans are in the fishing business. Crabs are their top seafood catch. Clams, sea bass, eels, and carp are also caught in Delaware waters. There are only about 100 miners in the state. Delaware stands last among the states in mining. Magnesium and sand and gravel are Delaware's leading minerals.

Overleaf: Rehoboth Beach

A Tour of the First State

A Tour of the First State

Recently, Delaware gained a new nickname: "Small Wonder." The state packs so much into so small a space. Delaware has beautiful beaches and woodlands. Many visitors enjoy the state's interesting towns and cities.

The Wilmington Area

Wilmington is a good place to begin a Delaware tour. It is in northern New Castle County. The city began near Fort Christina in 1638. Today, Wilmington has almost 72,000 people. It is Delaware's largest city.

Old Swedes Church

Old Swedes Church is a Wilmington landmark. Swedish people built it in 1698-99. It is one of the country's oldest Protestant churches still in use. The Delaware Art Museum is also in Wilmington. The museum has about 1,000 works by Delaware artist Howard Pyle. They include his wonderful painting called *The Mermaid*. Each fall, Wilmington hosts the Brandywine Arts Festival.

The du Ponts built many beautiful homes northwest of Wilmington. The first du Pont family

home is part of the Hagley Museum. The Eleutherian Mills are also there. These were Éleuthère Irénée du Pont's gunpowder mills. A schoolhouse, a barn, and gardens are other parts of the museum.

Henry Francis du Pont's home is now the Winterthur Museum and Gardens. Henry created lovely gardens around his nine-story home. The home's "period rooms" show how American houses looked at different times. Nemours Mansion and Gardens was Alfred I. du Pont's home. This 102-room mansion looks like a French king's palace. The

The first du Pont family home (above) is now part of the Hagley Museum.

The Eleutherian Mills

house is filled with furniture and paintings that date to the 1500s.

The Delaware Museum of Natural History is also northwest of Wilmington. The museum has one of the world's largest bird eggs. The 27-pound egg came from an elephant bird. That bird no longer exists. One of the world's largest clams can be seen there, too. This giant weighs 500 pounds.

OTHER NEW CASTLE COUNTY HIGHLIGHTS

The University of Delaware's Memorial Hall

Newark is southwest of Wilmington. Newark has nearly 26,000 people. That makes it the state's third-biggest city. The University of Delaware is in Newark. With about 20,000 students, it is the state's biggest school. The school's teams are called the Fightin' Blue Hens.

The Iron Hill Museum of Natural History is also at Newark. The museum is in a one-room schoolhouse. Fossils of ancient Delaware animals are displayed there. They include a mosasaur. This was a giant sea lizard. It lived 100 million years ago when Delaware was under water. The museum also has a replica of a Lenape village. In colonial times, iron was mined where the museum now stands. Today, visitors can walk into the old iron mine.

New Castle is south of Wilmington. Just under 5,000 people live there. Yet, it is one of America's most historic towns. The Dutch began it as Fort Casimir in 1651. New Castle was Delaware's first capital (1704-1777). Delaware lawmakers met in the Old Court House. The flags of four countries fly from that building—The Netherlands, Sweden, England, and the United States. Delaware has belonged to each of these countries at some time.

Amstel House is another New Castle landmark. This was the home of Nicholas Van Dyke. He governed Delaware from 1783 to 1786. George Washington was a wedding guest there in 1784. New Castle's Immanuel Church was begun in

The Old Court House in New Castle

A birds-eye view of Fort Delaware on Pea Patch Island

George Read was one of only six people who signed both the Declaration of Independence and the United States Constitution.

1703. It burned in 1980. When it was rebuilt, the surviving original walls were used and reinforced. Many famous Delawareans are buried in its churchyard. George Read is one of them. He signed the Declaration of Independence and the United States Constitution for Delaware.

Delaware City is south of New Castle. The Chesapeake and Delaware Canal is just south of the city. The canal connects Chesapeake Bay in Maryland to the Delaware River. The canal is a shortcut for ships. They carry goods to Philadelphia and across the Atlantic Ocean.

Boats carry visitors from Delaware City to Pea Patch Island. The island got its name from a tall tale. Supposedly, a boat carrying peas sank in the Delaware River. When the peas grew, they formed the island. Fort Delaware State Park is on the island. The fort was built in 1859. It is a pentagon-shaped building. It has five sides. During the Civil War, about 12,500 Confederate soldiers were imprisoned there. Today, visitors can explore their underground cells.

Odessa is southwest of Delaware City. Odessa's Corbit-Sharp House was built in 1774. The house shows how Americans lived between 1774 and 1818.

Fort Delaware

Kent County

Kent County covers the middle one-third of Delaware. Smyrna is just south of the county line. The town has many interesting homes. Belmont Hall is near Smyrna. It is more than 200 years old. Thomas Collins owned this mansion from at least 1753. During the Revolutionary War, the Collins family made bullets in the drawing-room fireplace. Later, Collins was Delaware's governor (1786-1789).

Bombay Hook National Wildlife Refuge is east of Smyrna. White geese called snow geese can be

Snow Geese at Bombay Hook National Wildlife Refuge

seen there. The refuge's wetlands also attract ducks and herons. Visitors might see diamondback terrapins there, too. These turtles have diamond-shaped patterns on their shells.

Dover is to the southwest. It is near Delaware's center. With nearly 28,000 people, Dover is Delaware's second-biggest city. In 1777, Dover replaced New Castle as Delaware's capital.

Delaware's capitol is called Legislative Hall. It looks like a big town hall. This is fitting for a small state. Its citizens often visit with their lawmakers. The Delaware Senate and House of Representatives meet on the first floor. Legislative Hall was finished

Legislative Hall is the name of Dover's capitol.

in 1933. It is one of the country's newest state capitols. Dover also has one of the country's oldest capitol buildings. The Old State House was built in 1792.

The Delaware State Museum is in Dover. The museum's Main Street, Delaware, re-creates an 1880s Delaware town. The museum also has old record players. Eldridge Johnson, a Dover man, helped develop this machine. He founded the Victor Talking Machine Company.

The Delaware Agricultural Museum and Village is also in Dover. Old farm buildings from around the state have been moved there. The museum has a log cabin from the 1600s.

Left: The Old State House
Right: Children with baby chicks at the Delaware Agricultural Museum

Dover Air Force Base is southeast of Dover. It is home to the country's largest cargo planes. The C-5 Galaxy is almost the length of a football field. Its tail stands six stories high. About 100 automobiles can be carried inside each C-5 Galaxy.

Harrington is south of Dover. Harrington hosts the Delaware State Fair each July. This ten-day fair has livestock and crop displays. Music and food are also offered. There is a Pretty Animal Contest. Children dress farm animals in clothing. Each child wears the same thing as his or her animal.

SUSSEX COUNTY

Delaware's southern one-third is in Sussex County. Slaughter Beach is just south of the county line. Each spring, the World Championship Weakfish Tournament takes place there. The people who land the heaviest weakfish win cash and prizes.

To the south is Lewes. In the early 1700s, pirates visited this Delaware Bay town. Blackbeard raided along the coast. Captain Kidd traded in Lewes. Stories are still told of sunken treasure off Lewes. Today, visitors go out on boats to watch for dolphins and whales. In 1931, the Zwaanendael Museum was built at Lewes. It marked the 300th

Carnival rides (above) and the Pretty Animal Contest (below) are highlights of the Delaware State Fair in Harrington.

anniversary of Delaware's first Dutch settlement. Visitors can learn about the early history of Lewes there.

Cape Henlopen Park is near Lewes. Each spring, it hosts the Delaware Kite Festival. Ocean and bay breezes make this a great place for kite flying.

Rehoboth Beach is south of Lewes. Many people from Washington, D.C., vacation there each summer. Rehoboth Beach has even been nicknamed the "Nation's Summer Capital." People sunbathe, sail, and water-ski in the area. In July, children enjoy the Rehoboth Beach Sandcastle Contest.

Georgetown is in the middle of Sussex County. Return Day is held there two days after Election Day. Winners and losers of city, state, and county elections gather together. They dress in colonial costumes. Then they ride together through the streets. They sit in horse-drawn carriages and old cars. This helps prevent hard feelings after elections. It also reminds people to work together for the good of Delaware.

Millsboro is south of Georgetown. Each fall, Nanticoke Indians meet there. They hold the Nanticoke Indian Powwow. Ceremonial dances are performed. Old stories are told. Indian crafts and

Dancers at the Nanticoke Indian Powwow

foods are enjoyed. Millsboro's Nanticoke Museum is a good place to learn about the Nanticoke people.

Trap Pond State Park is in southwestern Delaware. Part of Cypress Swamp covers this park. The country's largest stand of bald cypress trees is found there. People canoe and hike in the park. They also come to see the park's red-crested pileated woodpeckers.

To the south is Delmar. That is a good place to end a Delaware tour. This town is partly in Delaware and partly in Maryland. The elementary school is on the Maryland side. The high school is on the Delaware side. The Caboose is a railroad museum near Delmar. The museum is inside a real caboose.

Boys building a sandcastle at Seashore State Park

Overleaf: S. B. Woo

45

A Gallery of Famous Delawareans

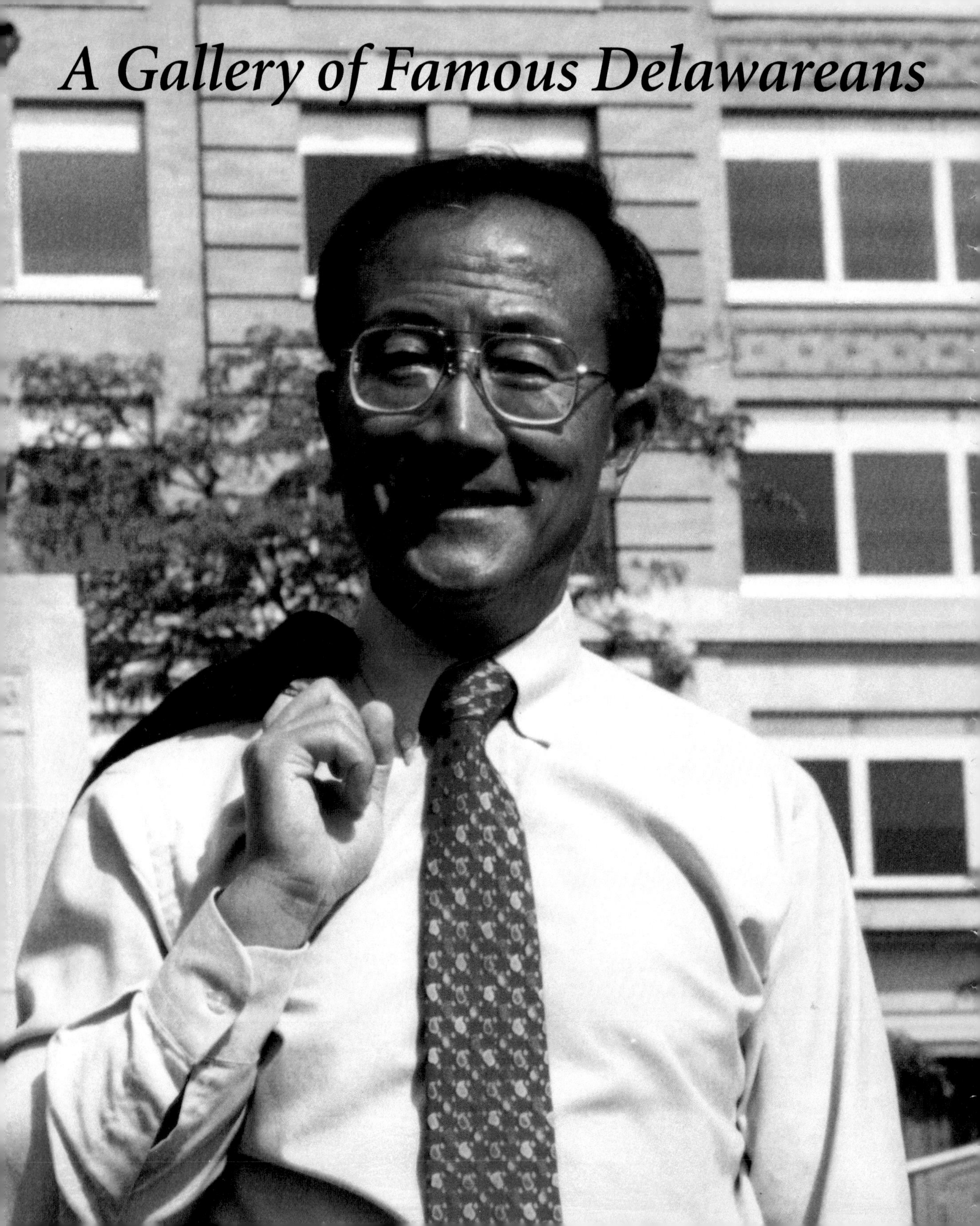

A Gallery of Famous Delawareans

Many Delawareans have left their mark on the world. They include lawmakers, writers, and an astronomer.

Caesar Rodney (1728-1784) was born near Dover. He had asthma. By the 1760s, he had cancer, too. Yet, he served Delaware in many ways. Rodney served in the colonial legislature. In 1776, he signed the Declaration of Independence for Delaware. To this day, his famous ride to Philadelphia is remembered. From 1778 to 1781, Rodney was Delaware's governor.

John Dickinson (1732-1808) was born in Maryland. When he was eight, his family moved to a plantation near Dover. Today, it is known as the John Dickinson Plantation. Later, he was a lawyer in Philadelphia, Pennsylvania. Before the Revolutionary War, Dickinson wrote many papers against English taxes. He was called the "Penman of the Revolution." Dickinson also fought in the Revolutionary War. After the war, he governed two states. Dickinson was the governor of Delaware (1781-1782) and the governor of Pennsylvania (1782-1785).

This statue of Caesar Rodney is at the U.S. Capitol in Washington, D.C.

Secretary of State Thomas Bayard (above) was the father of women's-rights worker Florence Bayard Hilles.

Thomas Bayard (1828-1898) was born in Wilmington. He became a famous statesman. He served as a U.S. senator from Delaware (1869-1885). From 1885 to 1889, he was U.S. secretary of state. Bayard was known for seeking peace between countries.

Oliver Evans (1755-1819) was born near Newport. As a boy, Evans read books about machines. By 1805, he had built a machine that moved over land. It was powered by steam. His machine was a forerunner of the automobile. Evans also invented a process that automated flour milling.

Richard Allen (1760-1831) was born a slave. He grew up on a plantation in Delaware. Allen taught himself to read and write. He became a preacher while he was still a slave. Reverend Allen saved enough money to buy his freedom in 1786. In 1787, he founded the African Methodist Episcopal church (AME) in Philadelphia. The AME was the country's first black church.

Mary Ann Shadd Cary (1823-1893) was from Wilmington. She founded schools for black people in Delaware and Pennsylvania. Later, she went to Canada. There, Cary aided black people who had fled from the United States. In 1854, she founded the *Provincial Freeman* newspaper in Canada. She was the first black woman in North America to become a newspaper editor. Cary was called "The Rebel." She also fought for women's voting rights.

Josephine Margaret Rebecca White (1849-1929) was also from Wilmington. She graduated from medical school in 1878. That made her one of Delaware's first woman doctors. Dr. White practiced medicine for fifty years in Wilmington. During that time, she cared for thousands of patients.

Emily Bissell (1861-1948) was born in Wilmington. Bissell designed the country's first Christmas seals. They were first sold at the Wilmington Post Office in 1907. Bissell also helped

The Christmas seals designed by Emily Bissell (below) were sold to raise money to fight tuberculosis.

Annie Jump Cannon

Daniel Nathans (on the left) won the 1978 Nobel Prize for medicine.

found the Delaware Art Museum. She began Wilmington's first free kindergarten, too. Besides all this, she started the city's first public playground.

Annie Jump Cannon (1863-1941) was born in Dover. She and her mother gazed at stars through an opening in their home's roof. Cannon became a famous astronomer. She showed that there are different kinds of stars. Cannon discovered 300 variable stars. The brightness of these stars changes over several years. Cannon is remembered as the "Census Taker of the Sky."

Belle Everett (1898-1989) was born in Maryland. She later moved to Delaware's Kent

County. Everett entered politics. In 1958, she was elected state treasurer. She was the first woman elected to state office in Delaware.

Daniel Nathans was born in Wilmington in 1928. He became a physician and medical researcher. Dr. Nathans' work has helped the treatment of cancer and other diseases. He won the 1978 Nobel Prize for medicine.

Howard Pyle (1853-1911) was born in Wilmington. He wrote and illustrated many children's books. *The Merrie Adventures of Robin Hood* was one of them. *The Story of King Arthur and His Knights* was another Pyle work. In 1900, he opened

Howard Pyle (right) did this illustration (left) for a book called Otto of the Silver Hand.

51

an art school in Wilmington. There, he taught many other artists.

John Marquand (1893-1960) and **Saunders Redding** (1906-1988) were both born in Wilmington. Marquand wrote novels. His book *The Late George Apley* won the 1938 Pulitzer Prize in fiction. Redding's books describe life among black Americans. *They Came in Chains* and *On Being Negro in America* are two of his works.

Helen Griffith was born in Wilmington in 1934. She wrote *Mine Will, Said John* and *Alex and the Cat*. Griffith is a children's author.

S. B. Woo was born in China in 1937. When he was eighteen, he came to America. Here Woo studied science. He became a physics teacher at the University of Delaware. He also entered politics. Between 1985 and 1989, he served as Delaware's lieutenant governor. Woo was the first Chinese-American to hold such a high office.

Katherine Ciesinski was born in 1950. **Kristine Ciesinski** came along two years later. Both were born in Wilmington. These sisters grew up to be opera singers. They are known worldwide.

Valerie Bertinelli was born in Wilmington in 1960. She became an actress. At fifteen, she was a television star. Bertinelli played kid-sister Barbara on

"One Day at a Time." She acted in this show until she was twenty-four.

The birthplace of Caesar Rodney, Oliver Evans, Emily Bissell, and Mary Ann Shadd Cary . . .

Home, too, of Richard Allen, John Dickinson, S. B. Woo, Belle Everett, and Éleuthère Irénée du Pont . . .

The place where America's first log cabins were built, where the U.S. Constitution was first approved, and where nylon was created . . .

Famous today for chemicals, broiler chickens, and peas . . .

This is the First State—Delaware!

Did You Know?

Several fossils were found in a group near Smyrna in 1992. They included whale, porpoise, and rhinoceros bones. Teeth from an 18-million-year-old chalicothere were also found. These were the first found on the East Coast from this horselike animal.

The *Bangor*, launched from Wilmington in 1844, was the nation's first oceangoing iron steamboat.

Delmar and Marydel are two towns that stretch across both Delaware and Maryland.

Delaware's northern border is curved. It is called the Twelve-Mile Circle. All the points along that part of the border are exactly 12 miles from the Old Court House in New Castle. They were marked in 1682. When the marks were connected by a line, part of a circle resulted.

In 1938, Delaware celebrated the 300th anniversary of the founding of Fort Christina (now Wilmington). The United States even minted a special half-dollar for the occasion. The front of the coin shows Wilmington's Old Swedes Church. The back shows a ship bringing the settlers to Delaware.

Belmont Hall, Governor Thomas Collins' home near Smyrna, is believed to have served briefly as Delaware's capitol building. The legislature may have met there at least once around 1790.

John Dickinson was a signer of the United States Constitution. Yet, he didn't sign his own name. Dickinson had to leave the meeting, so George Read signed for him.

Sulfa drugs have saved many lives. They are used to treat infectious diseases. In 1930, scientists in Wilmington made the first sulfa drugs in the United States.

Delaware schoolchildren convinced the legislature to name the ladybug the state bug in 1974.

In 1974, Wilmington native Dr. Henry J. Heimlich invented a way to help people who are choking. His Heimlich maneuver has saved over 35,000 lives in the United States alone.

Many people use mobile telephones today. This kind of phone was introduced at Wilmington in 1947 in a hookup between a car and an airplane.

The United States flag was reportedly first flown in the Battle of Cooch's Bridge in Delaware on September 3, 1777.

Delaware has towns named Bear, Red Lion, and Blackbird. Blue Ball, Gumboro, Pepperbox, Cabbage Corner, Cocked Hat, and Mermaid are other Delaware communities.

The space suits worn on the moon by United States astronauts were made in Delaware.

Delaware Information

State flag

Peach trees in bloom

Peach blossoms

Area: 2,044 square miles (only Rhode Island is smaller)

Greatest Distance North to South: 96 miles

Greatest Distance East to West: 39 miles

Borders: Pennsylvania to the north; New Jersey to the east across the Delaware River and Delaware Bay; the Atlantic Ocean to the southeast; Maryland to the south and west

Highest Point: 442 feet above sea level, in far northeastern Delaware

Lowest Point: Sea level, along the coast

Hottest Recorded Temperature: 110° F. (at Millsboro, on July 21, 1930)

Coldest Recorded Temperature: -17° F. (also at Millsboro, on January 17, 1893)

Statehood: The first state, on December 7, 1787

Origin of Name: The name *Delaware* honors Thomas West, Lord De La Warr, the first colonial governor of Virginia

Capital: Dover (since 1777)

Earlier Capital: New Castle (1704-1777)

Counties: 3

United States Senators: 2

United States Representatives: 1

State Senators: 21

State Representatives: 41

State Song: "Our Delaware," by George Hynson (words) and William Brown (music)

State Motto: "Liberty and Independence"

Nicknames: "First State," "Diamond State," "Blue Hen State," "Small Wonder"

State Seal: Adopted in 1777

State Flag: Adopted in 1913

State Flower: Peach blossom

State Bird: Blue hen chicken

State Tree: American holly

State Bug: Ladybug

State Fish: Weakfish

State Mineral: Sillimanite

State Colors: Colonial blue and buff

Some Rivers: Delaware, Brandywine Creek, Christina, Smyrna, St. Jones, Nanticoke, Pocomoke

Wildlife: Deer, foxes, beavers, rabbits, muskrats, otters, snapping turtles, diamondback terrapins, horseshoe crabs, weakfish, clams, crabs, sturgeon, bass, eels, carp, pickerel, many other kinds of fish, woodpeckers, orioles, snowy egrets, blue herons, hawks, ducks, cardinals, many other kinds of birds

Manufactured Products: Chemicals, medicines, food products, paper products, rubber products, plastic goods, automobiles, scientific instruments

Farm Products: Broiler chickens, hogs, milk, green peas, soybeans, corn, apples, barley, wheat, potatoes, flowers, shrubs

Fishing Products: Crabs, clams, sea bass, eels, carp

Mining Products: Sand and gravel, magnesium

Population: 666,168, forty-sixth among the fifty states (1990 U.S. Census Bureau figures)

Major Cities (1990 Census):

Wilmington	71,529	Seaford	5,689
Dover	27,630	Smyrna	5,213
Newark	25,098	New Castle	4,837
Milford	6,040	Middletown	3,834
Elsmere	5,935	Georgetown	3,732

Blue hen chickens

Holly

Ladybugs

Delaware History

8000 B.C.—The first people probably reach Delaware

A.D. 500—American Indians are living in Delaware

1400—The Lenape arrive in Delaware

1609—English explorer Henry Hudson explores Delaware Bay for the Netherlands

1631—The Dutch found Zwaanendael at present-day Lewes

1632—Zwaanendael is destroyed by Indians

1638—Swedish colonists found New Sweden; a permanent settlement is begun at Fort Christina

1643—Johan Printz arrives to govern New Sweden

1651—The Dutch build Fort Casimir at present-day New Castle

1655—The Dutch capture New Sweden, which becomes part of New Netherland

1664—The English seize New Netherland; Delaware becomes an English colony

1682—Delaware is attached to Pennsylvania as the "Three Lower Counties"

1698—Old Swedes Church is built at Wilmington

1704—The Three Lower Counties are granted their own separate legislature

1717—Dover is laid out

1767-68—John Dickinson protests English taxes in several articles

1775-1783—More than 3,500 Delawareans help the United States win independence in the Revolutionary War

1776—Caesar Rodney, George Read, and Thomas McKean sign the Declaration of Independence for Delaware; the Three Lower Counties become the Delaware State

1777—The English win the Battle of Cooch's Bridge near Newark

1785—The *Delaware Gazette*, Delaware's first known newspaper, is published at Wilmington

1787—Delaware becomes the "First State" on December 7 by adopting the U.S. Constitution before any other state

1802—Éleuthère Irénée du Pont begins a gunpowder mill that becomes Wilmington's giant Du Pont Company

1829—The Chesapeake and Delaware Canal opens from Maryland to eastern Delaware

1833—The University of Delaware is founded as Newark College

1861-65—More than 12,000 Delawareans help the North win the Civil War

1887—Happy 100th birthday, First State!

1897—Delaware's present constitution is adopted

1899—The Delaware Corporation Law is passed, making it easier for businesses to be formed in Delaware than elsewhere

1911-24—The Du Pont Highway is built

1917-18—Nearly 10,000 Delawareans serve in World War I

1923—Cecile Steele begins Delaware's broiler chicken industry

1929-39—The Great Depression puts thousands of Delawareans out of work

1933—Legislative Hall, Delaware's state capitol, is completed

1941-45—Delaware sends about 30,000 men and women to help win World War II

1951—The Delaware Memorial Bridge opens, linking Delaware to New Jersey

1963—Delaware outlaws racial segregation in restaurants

1971—Delaware passes the Coastal Zone Act to prevent large factories from being built along the coast

1981—The Financial Center Development Act is passed to encourage out-of-state banks to move to Delaware

1987—Happy 200th birthday, First State!

1990—Delaware's population is 666,168

Civilian Conservation Corps (CCC) workers at Slaughter Beach during the Great Depression

MAP KEY

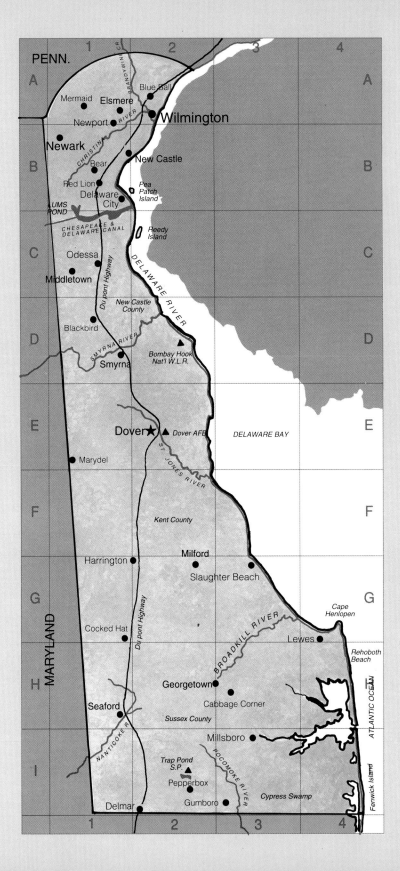

GLOSSARY

ancient: Relating to a time long ago

caboose: The last car of a train

canal: A waterway built to link two bodies of water

capital: The city that is the seat of government

capitol: The building in which the government meets

climate: The typical weather of a region

coast: Land along a large body of water

colony: A settlement outside a parent country that is ruled by the parent country

constitution: A framework of government

depression: A period of widespread joblessness

desegregate: To end the process of keeping the races apart

explorer: A person who visits and studies unknown lands

financial: Relating to banks and money

fossil: The remains of an animal or a plant that lived long ago

industry: A large business activity that employs many workers

legislature: A lawmaking body

million: A thousand thousand (1,000,000)

nylon: A strong material invented at the Du Pont Company in 1938

peninsula: Land almost completely surrounded by water

pentagon: A five-sided figure or building

population: The number of people living in a place

powwow: A get-together of American Indians

replica: A copy or model of something

segregation: The process of keeping people of different races apart

slavery: A practice in which some people own other people

tourism: The business of providing such services as food and lodging for travelers

wildlife refuge: A place where animals are protected

Azalea Woods at Winterthur Gardens, Wilmington

PICTURE ACKNOWLEDGMENTS

Front cover, © **Kevin Fleming**; 1, © **Kevin Fleming**; 2, **Tom Dunnington**; 3, © **Kevin Fleming**; 4-5, **Tom Dunnington**; 6-7, © **Tom Till**; 8, © **Gene Ahrens**; 9 (top), **Courtesy of Hammond, Incorporated, Maplewood, New Jersey**; 9 (bottom), © Mary A. Root/**Root Resources**; 10, © C. Postmus/**Root Resources**; 11, © **W. J. Talarowski/N E Stock Photo**; 12, **The Hagley Museum and Library, Wilmington**; 13, **Archives & Manuscripts Division of the Oklahoma Historical Society**; 14, **PNC Bank, Delaware, Robert E. Goodier, A.W.S., W.H.S., artist**; 15, © William Talarowski/ **N E Stock Photo**; 16, © **Cameramann International, Ltd.**; 17, © **J.L.G. Ferris, Archives of 76, Bay Village, Ohio**; 18, © **Mary Ann Brockman**; 20, **Hagley Museum & Library**; 21, **Delaware State Archives, Dover, Delaware**; 22 (top), **Courtesy of the Historical Society of Delaware**; 22 (bottom), © **Kevin Fleming**; 23, **Delaware State Archives, Dover, Delaware**; 24 (left), **AP/Wide World Photos**; 24 (right), **Delaware State Archives, Dover, Delaware**; 25 (both pictures), **AP/Wide World Photos**; 27, © **W.J. Talarowski/N E Stock Photos**; 28, © **Kevin Fleming**; 29 (top), © **Kevin Fleming**; 29 (bottom), © **Wm. Talarowski/N E Stock Photos**; 30 (top), © **Kevin Fleming**; 30 (bottom), © **Cameramann International, Ltd.**; 31, © **Kevin Fleming**; 32-33, © **Jim Pickerell/Tony Stone Images, Inc.**; 34, © **W.J. Talarowski/N E Stock Photo**; 35 (top), © **Robert J. Bennett/Photri, Inc.**; 35 (bottom), © **Kevin Fleming**; 36, © **Kevin Fleming**; 37, © **Mary Ann Brockman**; 38, © **Kevin Fleming**; 39, © **Lani/Photri, Inc.**; 40, © **Kevin Fleming**; 41, © **Mae Scanlan**; 42 (left), © **Mary Ann Brockman**; 42 (right), © **Wm. Talarowski/N E Stock Photo**; 43 (both pictures), © **Robert J. Bennett/ Photri, Inc.**; 44, © **Photri, Inc.**; 45, © **Wm. Talarowski/N E Stock Photo**; 46, **Courtesy S. B. Woo**; 47, **Courtesy of the Historical Sockety of Delaware**; 48, **Stock Montage, Inc.**; 49, **Courtesy of the Historical Society of Delaware**; 50 (top), **Harvard College Observatory**; 50 (bottom), **AP/Wide World Photos**; 51 (left), **Delaware Art Museum, Howard Pyle Collection**; 51 (right), **Courtesy of the Historical Society of Delaware**; 53 (left), **AP/Wide World Photos**; 53 (right), **UPI/Bettmann**; 54 (top), **Courtesy of the Museum of the American Numismatic Association**; 54 (bottom), **The Mariners' Museum, Newport News, Virginia**; 55, **NASA**; 56 (top), **Courtesy Flag Research Center, Winchester, Massachusetts 01890**; 56 (middle), © **Robert J. Bennett/Photri, Inc.**; 56 (bottom), © **Kohout Productions/Root Resources**; 57 (top), **Delaware Department of Agriculture**; 57 (middle), © **Kitty Kohout/Root Resources**; 57 (bottom), © **Jerry Hennen**; 59, **Courtesy of the Historical Society of Delaware**; 60, **Tom Dunnington**; 62, © **Gene Ahrens**; back cover, © **W.J. Talarowski/N E Stock Photo**

INDEX

Page numbers in boldface type indicate illustrations.

ABOUT THE AUTHORS

Dennis and Judith Fradin have coauthored several books in the From Sea to Shining Sea series. The Fradins both graduated from Northwestern University in 1967. Dennis has been a professional writer for twenty years, and has published 150 books. His works for Childrens Press include the Young People's Stories of Our States series, the Disaster! series, and the Thirteen Colonies series. Judith earned her M.A. in literature from Northwestern University and taught high-school and college English for many years. The Fradins, who are the parents of Anthony, Diana, and Michael, live in Evanston, Illinois.